Paperwhite

Paperwhite

Catherine Mamo

thistledown press

Thistledown Press Ltd.
633 Main Street
Saskatoon, Saskatchewan, S7H 0J8
www.thistledownpress.com

Library and Archives Canada Cataloguing in Publication

Mamo, Catherine, 1964–
Paperwhite / Catherine Mamo.

Poems.
ISBN 978-1-897235-60-7

I. Title.

PS8626.A48 P36 2009   C811'.6   C2009-900760-6

Cover photograph: ©Gregor Schuster/zefa/Corbis
Cover and book design by Jackie Forrie
Printed and bound in Canada

10 9 8 7 6 5 4 3 2 1

Canada Council   Conseil des Arts
for the Arts   du Canada

SASKATCHEWAN
ARTS BOARD

Canadian   Patrimoine
Heritage   canadien

Thistledown Press gratefully acknowledges the financial assistance of the Canada Council for the Arts, the Saskatchewan Arts Board, and the Government of Canada through the Book Publishing Industry Development Program for its publishing program.

For Michael: through thick and thin . . .

Contents

Breeding Lilacs

The Picket Fence

Ma

Filmy Sleep

The Cruelest Month

Dizzying the new
butterflies testing the air.

They work hard
to move their beauty
then recover, heating themselves
on stone, communicating
their electric pulse
through time, fossilizing
some idea of themselves.

As reliable are the sandhill
cranes; the tired eddies
of their long wingbeats,
and their talk, that eerie warbling,
drifts toward the earth
in locked code,
writing the necessity
of their navigations
on the barren ground.

Flickers chase one another
through slim white birches.
Yellow fritillaries, spring beauties,
and waxy buttercups flatter hillsides
still dull with unbirthed soil.

Why is nature
so quick to rebirth
while we, morbid egoists,
whither in our cocoons

as all around us
the earth pulses

begin begin begin . . .

April II

why do children
keep arriving

why do they swing and laugh

why does the grass
bend its one colour so

The highstrung horses
now have a madness
put upon them
as an excess of light
molecule by molecule
enters
the elemental eye
the velvet snout

The earth
has circled again
and all must
either live or die

but who
decides

Thirst

It's a thirst so violent
and elemental
you wake midnight
knocking things over
to reach the glass,
yet you cannot slake
or outrun it.
Then dream of leaning
down to clear running water,
drinking with your face
like bear or deer
tongue lapping
at the very origins,
the very continuance.
But there's fear here also,
invisible chemical encodings;
what can be seen
through microscopes calmly
swimming in your goblet.
And, why not, a skull
that deeper reflection
of the face?
Unlike Narcissus
you shall not drown here
or become a flower.
Then the river is frozen.
You cannot
break the surface
anymore,
and the thirst becomes this
animal, itself liquid,
exquisitely furred.

You lie in wait
aim your eye barrel,
but it slips through
trembling human hands,
evaporates to cloud —
a wispy summer mare's tail
and you wake holding this
scribble: *It's not a thirst of the body*

There is Always a Lawnmower

chewing up the long
May evenings,
making the nestlings
tremble.

How did we become,
suburban halflings, so
indentured to our plot
of thin soil
and dandelions
to work our fingers thus
past sundown,
smothered in lilac
scented evening

while the two beasts
of our middle age
lie sleeping in our breasts

Listening to Gould

A cat could play those keys
but rarely
A broken June
what mould
should not be smashed
in order
to create anew
Creaking by shadow
precious ones
off to land of nod
and I cannot forget
for one second
the scent of them
This cave our house
so full of whats
brought back from the hunt
mammoth bones
arranged to full effect
the ikebana
the trailing ivy
soon we will
have to move
so our stuff will have more room
Now the radio man lists
a litany of horrors
perpetrated
human upon human
but no balm
the storm whips up
to placate
the swollen
ovary   no only
people dying
for/on another speck

of ground
and have my beans sprouted?
You know I care
but prefer to bite
my own tail
and worry my existence
so sacredly given
to mute anthropological remains:
Cave Woman
artifact #3,452
who stares at me through glass
and why?

A Visit to Kathryn, Alberta

Where the swing swings itself
continuously against the continuous
horizon

Where the wind
gasps at the windows
children in the pitch of fever
moan, wrung like rags,
their bodily fluids
discharged to the four directions

Microscopic enemy
big prairie sky

We take what the weather
deals out like the lichen
covered stones,
the meadowlarks, the mud

This landscape eludes —
too thirsty, with bovine
countenance
A blackbird offers its white eyes
for a song,
its broken wing for love

The virus thickens
our blood
We curl into
isolettes of skin
and under the hammering hail
dream

Voice of the killdeer
high and strange

Eloise, Rendered

We found her
in a sage hollow
above White Lake,
stinking to heaven,
becoming an ecosystem,
her ribcage a globe,
coated in paltry leather.

Visiting her from time to time
we witnessed her disintegration:
parts slowly carried off.

This time, nothing left
but some vertebrae, a femur
and the great, gaping pelvis:
the passage her calves
slipped through
when she was still
grazing here among us —
sun upon her broadness.

Laundry Meditation

Take the Japanese cup
fill with hot ginger tea

Forget that you are dying

Let Vishwa Mohan take you down
to the river with his
Hindu blues

Thirsty ears   Thirsty ears

Obtain a stable position
Approach the laundry mountain

The loved ones abed
their daily demolitions
cleared away

From what far away planet
a spy looks down,
sees a woman tenderly
folding each piece of her family
into neat clean squares

Then speak
of the emptiness
that is full

The wild strumming
men play on
and you have travelled

A cut branch stuck in water
leafs out

As Rumi says

*There are hundreds of ways
to kneel and kiss the ground.*

Crocodile Meditation

I am blood
temperature
in the tepid
continuity
of things

Have gnawed
my share of greatness —
leg of eland
leg of lion

but the prey
is nothing

It's just that I've lain
forever thus

rounded parts submerged
not a single scale or toe
exposed

Island I am
of beastly teeth
ceaselessly hunting
eyes
staring down

the same patch of coloured tile
the rubber duck

Scar

We all have a party trick.
Mine is showing off
the puckered jellyfish scar
under my left arm, received
when a Portuguese Man-O-War
tried to embrace and drown me
in the Mediterranean sea

(if a floating mass of jelly can be said to "try" anything)

I may have been feeling a lot
like a jelly fish — brainless, see through, watery
when my arm swam into a tentacle;
just the tip of the toe of it.
(The beast could have been 30 feet long
I later learned.)

Searing pain shot in.
I lit out for shore, screaming;
the man I was with swam even faster.

He tried to make up
for his cowardice by trying to suck the sting out.
I hope my poison's still in him.

My arm swelled, blistered and bled.
It became a knife wound for a while
until I realized the truth was stranger, better.

A few months after, I found one
marooned on the beach, collapsed, harmless.
"You're out of your element old chum" I said
and sat with him a while, worrying my new scar.

Hum #1

where's there to fly to?
only here   universe of the skull

terrorizing amusing
memorizing ourselves
tripping through
the accumulated bone baggage
what encrusts
cements the open core

we become concretions
flesh into stone

there beyond the mysterious mountain
the same — chewable vitamins
bloom of the lipstick plant

so what is the obstacle
between the tree and me?
between you and me?
made of the same ingredients
mist and dirt
we look at things
we eat   we cry we die

forgetting
noticing forget
embracing
relating
dowsing intent
betraying fear

stay put
have courage
drop real and unreal
good and bad
so that with love we may proceed —
grow
to man and woman

Hum #2

How, if some day or night a demon were to sneak after you into your loneliest loneliness and say to you, "This life as you now live it and have lived it, you will have to live it once more and innumerable times more . . ."

— Nietzsche

How alive
  How listening

Nosing along
like Wodwo
creating darkness

Meshed voices
churning far away
 in the one energy
                light
    in the moon

Why you
   of all eons

      circling grey water

           whore
         of temporary fictions
believer in nothing

Why you
   given the voice

no one can hear?

So we exist
   what next?

Grow a life
   that's nowhere twice

Fish

In a river dream we nose
the smooth current   rooting
for love in a wake
of eggs and sperm

In all this water
how thirsty

More than primitive
in our scales
our minds move as one wave
one elemental surge
pulsing pulsing onward

From splendid red
to this living mottled rot
our biological necessity
to be eaten from the inside out

The fish beside me bares his teeth
Dying and not happy
he grabs my tail and takes me with him
back over the falls
for one last chance
one last arc into the teeth of death
to throw ourselves onto rock
and into
the next generation

After We Made Love on a Rock by the Red Deer River

we shared a warm plum, slept
for a while like the innocent
forgotten few
while swallows
spiraled high
and tangled wings,
plummeted,
scooping sky
between their feathers.

The milky tea river
kept on, full of dead
and dying crickets.
They too had made the exchange,
clutching the grass blade,
then falling together
in furious embrace.

It was September,
still hot in the badlands;
bleaching the bones of summer,
silvering
the cottonwood limbs,
the sage by thirst
split open.

We watched flies
drink our mingled fluids,
plunging their tongues
in the pool of our love,

and belonged for a while
to the turning of things.

Chant

In time
   the tired fog will lift
     and eerily swallows will alight
drifted from shores unknown

In time
   that honeyed light will slip
again sideways
   through the shafts of grasses
warm the vessels
   the tongues the mildewed grooves

In time
   my boy will step
into hand me down shoes and go —
   he will not glance back

In time
   I will have time
to follow myriad lifeforms again
   to study each step   methodical
as a February stinkbug
   minding the sill shaking each limb
mild and purposeful
   as rain

The Butterfly Poacher

You had begun to trust again,
painfully, slowly changing inside
the spun chrysalis of Self.
Your mother was free:
blue and lilting, wild, born
among the honed down bones of mountains.
Your father was love himself, Eros,
of the body.
They met at night and made you,
secret and divine as light, though
you never knew it until
the sudden strange moment
of metamorphosis
when the grey casing split
and your hair, the long
still pale wrinkled wings,
emerged like morning glory petals,
spun with dew and sun glance,
But this was not your home;
not the alpine meadow
huddled between ragged peaks,
formed of crushed together
continents and the praying hands
of women. Butterfly: the female soul, *Psyche*,
passing from life to life, awakening,
opening your eyes
in the den of the poacher.
He peers down through thick glasses,
breath humid and oniony.
The pin descends
glinting.

The Change Room

celestial blue walls
and a somehow Mediterranean light
upon them

the tittering of girls
like the harmonics of
butterflies

the musk of their youth
in the damp heat of midsummer
as around brown toes
bikinis fall

they shower off
chlorine soap and all
that life has given them
for they are lovely but don't
know it

where they stand
with dark hair rivering
down their backs
bare arms raised like caryatids

in this brief holding
space between the beaten sun
and the eyes of the predators

for their wants
will trample the world
but not yet
not yet

Summer Variations

1.

Scorched summer —
   even the crickets
are choking of thirst
   in the singed fields
and the brittle leaves
   answer like water

Heaviness of noon
   on the cut hay
Crow loiter —
   the plain shadow
lies lengthwise across August
   cut out of cured leather
and the hunger
   of the young

What once were streams
   kick up dust and smoke
as the tall fire leaps
   closer in the night
eats the moon out of spite

2.

Amphibean summer —
   submerged, water in the ear canal
the roar of underness, dive through
   weedy caravans, frog legs catching
   at the frills
   Shocking to minnows the white
human moving there
   Cool pebbles, well rested,
hope for more eons to sleep through
   under the eye of trout
Piled up cumulus
   tinged with strange violet, but that sky

and those dry hills
        no longer my element, aquatic now,
    half crocodilian eyes above
  into the hot wind
      cottonwoods wild and soundless
          as I ride the underbellies of waves

3.

Brain of moonshine
        lust and sleep
    In the heat
we are fluff
    white butterflies at play
        the music of other lands
      a baby's catapulting senses
      green water   fish moving slow
Ungainly on land
    we slouch   unreal
aching to be heard
    worrying the bones of love
The wind can fester
        into all corners
            Then who decides
            what lives what dies

4.

Twilight swaddling the hills
    Summer drifts
on the laughter of girls
    spent berries dropping
            bear grunt

The half moon edge
    slicing bright
    dragonflies hunt through

Somewhere down
   in that evergreen valley
our children sleep
   in rooms of blue and cinnamon

5.

A moment between
   in the blank dust of August
naked as the cherry tree
   savaged by toddlers,
crimson stains
   down tanned forearms

Dead like the cicada
   silenced by the water pail
the gangrenous crow, Poe
      maimed named and claimed
   just stuck his black claws up in the air
He had not seen one season
   on this dangerous planet

Green depressions
   filled with pointless anxieties
glimpses of chaos
   amongst all our tidy eventualities
the nothing objects

So this is summer
      murderous adulterous
fabulous and brief

Poem for Michael

Husband
I want to learn you
again

Unhinge you
with simple
tenderness

This decade of kisses
has swept us along
like the storm we laid down
to watch fly
over our garden

wind shivering
the foundation

lightning bolts seared
on our eye sockets

sky switching
on and off

We talked about electricity
while the babies slept
and you said:

> If only we could remember
> that we are always new

Today could be
our turning
and I want
to turn with you
laughing at the same jokes
inventing new ones

as the next thousand years
begins on earth

While You Were Away

I slept with
the moon
that rock of light

Lusted after every
tanned arm hanging out
a car window

Flew with crows
into the lap
of a cool green forest

Forgave the children
their birth and
banished
my own bones

Delved like a worm
into unnecessary tunnels

Caught a summer whinny
off the snout
of a fallow horse

Into the meteor of a cat's eye

Heard doves coo the long evening
into stars

While you were away
I ate hot buttered beans
licked my fingers
clean

The Picket Fence

We have it all
the boy the girl the house
with lake and mountain views
a fine marriage
(without the paperwork)
and yes
even a picket fence

Scavenged from the dump —
not white anymore
a little bent
stuck in the garden for
wabi sabi
the soul of worn down things

It's a fragment from
someone else's ideal life
tossed on the scrap heap

replaced with chainlink

A humble fence
marker of nothing
thrower of thin
shadows

Trip

Place of lazy green river
fish suspended
only an occasional
silver glimmer

Even the children
tricked
into a thick sleep
like pebbles
mindful

We walk over
the Doukhobor dead
gathering faded
petals of cloth
the wind had eaten

Silence under us
A road ahead
A road behind

We comb the teeth
of darkness and shake out
two nits —
girl child   boy child

They come
all naked need
and howling
so we take them up

begin this history

Tom's Lesson

I need you to remind me:

We won't ever have a day
like this one again mama

Never again the exact slant
of light on sheen of mallard

The skeleton of a leaf
discovered among pebbles

Never again the exact
mundane pleasure of sorting socks

while you play and sing
limbs brazen with life
amazed with your own being

Three whole years of wisdom
and you remind me

   never a day like this

Life by Rote

My hands have memorized their duties
stirring the porridge
turning the baby

With a pianist's span
they are manly, besilvered

The wrists belong
to a smaller person
someone delicate and prone
to fevers

My hands know
how to turn keys make braids plant sunflowers
find their way around
the landscape of him

Though competent they
are often tempted
to danger —
into the blender's spinning blades
under hammers just to see
into a vacuum to feel the pull

and then they write things
perhaps they shouldn't
pointing out the devious
familiarity of it all

Envy and What It Comes Round To

I want to do Tai Chi
under the Tamarind tree
like people in glossy
travel magazines

ride a dugout canoe
up the Amazon

let my boots
hike me up peaks
of serene magnitude
again

but we are anchored
to this kitchen table

The children peer
over their bowls of soup,
eyes glinting and expectant
as distant rivers

So I make a monkey face
and we have a laugh

That's how I return to them
always

After lunch
they climb me
like a Tamarind tree

Daughter

you are not
a consumer

you are not
a target audience

you are not
the clothes you wear

you are not
the latest gadget

you are you are

the ground of being

incarnation
of a slave girl

queen of the dust motes

a highwire act

one of Shiva's arms

a green shoot

Aster
heart of a flower

Rummaging

I like the sound of that —
to dig through
expectantly
but we are closed
now no scent of baking
through the screen door
for bears to lap
just
a few wild strawberries
and little water
the animals must
press on
wind swoops
over the thicket
where they snooze
mama and cub
that mother love
I know too
look at all they have learned

sighing shadows
over the solstice hump
limping towards summer
dryness distraction wind
characterize this June
as his foot nods to nonexistent
music
the length of him
washed in lamplight

I'd do it all again little demon
yes in fact I would

I'd lean again
into the orange poppy buzz
that on the hummingbird's chest
marks its way

we each have
our mountain to climb
to stand and look from
the top   still alive and
kicking or just alive see
those years stretch behind and those before
and we are
the intersection

Visit of the Hover Fly

She's mad for the dill,
knows each floret
intimate, carnal,
abdomen pulsing, plunger
tongue reaching the stamen and licking,
eyes eclipsed by yellow.

Utter absorption
in the object of desire.

Her day is this voyage
round and round the dill flower,
adoring it from every angle
sucking every dewdrop
cleaning her legs in flight.

Unaware of the strangeness of her own making;
hummingbird wing technique,
constant motion
disguise of wasp,
millions of years of evolution
so she could hover here at my picnic table
July 10, 2005, 7:30 am.

Intimations

of the end

enigmatic
witherings

hungry hatching moths

that toy
with a hatchet
and a killing gleam

a bird lays down
its wings before me;
he has it down
to the dead eye

then the old woman
stunned immobile
as the water seeps
into her car

neighbour
had a heart attack
in the garden;
her husband with alzheimer's
didn't remember
he had a wife

light hidden
both sun and moon
by a skim of cloud

humans live here;
thin layer between
the bubbling core
and the toxic ether

one solemn girl
upon a grey horse

Blue River

More rain
in the blue dusk   amplified
in the incandescence
of one lamp under which sun
our heroine
scratches the page

She is entering
the middle years
wearing her thickness
her long straight life
like a tired garment

She looks up
listening as trumpets
blare through — little Bach fairies
touching up brass
Brass; what she could never be called,
retiring behind thick lenses,
mishapen retinas
and baggy corduroy

Cord du roi; something of the king,
always something, one word
unknown, one gesture
one gentle unseen shift
one leap into the breathless
sky emptying

Rain at Blue River

Time Time Time
the tide, the bird —
a woman's wish
wearing wings

Lost Poem

Thought the poem,
lost the poem.

Now it belongs to the fire-wind
blowing the dead smell
into some creature's nostrils

Or the spilling
summer light that crowns
the grasses and beatifies
all
the simple and not
so simple
organisms
bending
to time and wind

Evening upon the dry ridges

A change approaches —
be alert
be kind

remember

Ma

Babies babies
born out of a dead cow's eye.
Nothing can stop them
from tearing into this world —
not war, not famine, not grief,
not even the shriveling of the love
that made them.

They come too pink
and needy, to be gathered like stalks,
like blooms of unfortunate beauty.

Ravens ravens
born out of my dead eye,
the glass eye in the bottom
of my teacup. A storm brews there;
all that was known, now forgotten,
the lonely looking in
lit windows, the shreds
of dreams, the clear of the eye,
the hard white,
the green ferris wheel,
the vertiginous pupil
and that other
dark pool
out of which emerged
that first strangled
elemental word, the brash caw
sounding

Ma.

I am a Lazy Wife

I sleep like winter:
coiled, immaculate

I will not give birth
I am too tired
to pass myself on

I move ponderously
in our house, like something
doomed for extinction

My sleep is precious,
a fossilized shell

I encompass
the void, the drunken scent
of rotten fruit

Another page
flies off the calendar
The wind reminds me
of someone invisible and fierce

I have my talents:
waiting, listening, wanting

I want, I want
to enter a fish's gullet
and swim there,
tiny as that again,
where we came from,
like light, like sound

I want, I want
to wither with the plants
and drop away
as autumn comes tumbling and rain
fills our bed

Autumn

and an empty road
inspires the mad woman
to sing

her crooked song
fills me with love;
this is the sweet demeanor
of knowinglessness.

Her bruised, abandoned eyes
filter what she cannot.

I've seen her in town,
carrying a six pack, returning empties,
once licking an ice cream
in summer among the children.

Her sunned hair sways,
animal
her solitary progress.

A man in a purple car
stops to offer her a lift;
from behind she's a girl,
blonde, blue-jeaned.

Her face slowly turning
is a shock; warped,
absent and serene
like he'll never comprehend.

Her song halts
at her lips,
like a butterfly
pinned.

AWAKE!

Coyotes howl like ambulances.
Limbs, dense with exhaustion
tingle, prick awake like stars
or puncturing teeth.

Long tear of the canines.
They are starving dogs in this heat,
picking off the weak.

I may have stolen someone else's life;
princess of the briars,
eating dried berries off the stem,
all tongue and stomach,
voice gone or stolen, blood
licked clean and the beauty
deadened.

So we begin to feel our age
in the long hours of darkness,
like some terrible prophecy at last
revealing itself as the vapour
on the mirror clears.

The sun continues its work,
beating down indifferently
on skin, feathers, rock
or brain with its incessant merry-go-round
amusements; peering forwards, spelunking
the murk

for somewhere
is the diamond
or a glittering bone, an opening
onto

Good Morning Ganesh

The pink wash
of morning spreads

Our town blinks
and the motors begin

Nothing like the clamour
of life on the Ganges

Where wild dogs gnaw
on charred corpses

Men women children cows
all bathing in the sacred muck

Offering thanks down to the crumb
each lentil given to continue

Or is it so very
different

When both rich and poor
dangle
from your prayer wheel

and your elephant eyes
troll our lives

Searching for Myself in a Ravine

I know I passed this way;
left a long fair hair
on the tall grasses,
the flower footprint
of my sole in the muck,
tasted a winter apple
from the tired orchard,
remembered an olive grove
and a boy tasting of olives, there
the impression of our summered limbs.
Bushes impinge, blackberry briars
place where girls are murdered
and left to be
found by happy dogs.
Perhaps I am there white
toes pointing to a final sleep.
But I had a cellphone and self-defense,
have escaped rape —
that nasty frenchman
plied upon mine his fishy mouth
and I spit and kicked,
slithered out the car window.
Streak of wildness
with town circling, hungry.
Here I stopped,
did a *Sound of Music* twirl,
took in what humanity has made
while considering the boy's question
how many layers does the earth have?
(the giant jawbreaker),
augered into the ground,
rose up angelic
in a beam of light,
or returned to pick up my son
from swimming at two.

September

We are readying:
Cats move indoors
replete with summer's hunt,
blood stained paws,
burrs in their coats,
quilts come out
of their plastic wrap,
fire evacuation suitcases
unpacked for finally
the rain.

I wear an apron
covered in flour, grab a moment
to read of the Lady of the Haystacks;
delirious in some English field,
setting up house with grass snakes and mice.

She was soon committed
of course . . .

But we've all dreamt of a place,
cave cabin or haystack,
away from chores, bills, taxes, and toilet bowls
to clean where somehow
enlightenment will befall us
in the loneliness of a golden autumn,
as though the skin could suddenly burst
like a ripe pod and the heart seeds
scatter, given enough silence
and the extremities of undivided time,
plus a touch of madness;
gift of the cow sacrificed
upon the altar of supper.

September and the burnt
mountain sighs.
To tend to the dough
I rise.

Fall Poem

Deer may or may not
be falling
but the gunshots
ring
out.

(See the mare's tail
clouds tinged with violet)

Walk soft
the forest doesn't mind.

You give nothing much
recalling the too small
motions of a day: a reach, a lick,
a push, a stroke.

It's just the way
of the turning leaf,
it's things landing
in your coffee.

Some poor farmer picked it.

Such fine, wrinkled hands,
such hands as chop and stack.

As the wood splits, crack,
as it gives way and becomes two,
as the deer falls and
becomes nothing

her deep eyes
blink their last.

Cows in the Cemetery

They have found
their Elysian fields —
pastures of the dead,
fresh wreaths and
centuries of green.

A gravestone shivers
or have my eyes gone
crooked from fever?

Does the blue spruce
reach out its stubby, prickly limbs
imploring me
to rest,
to lie with another
Catherine and her brood;
their names gone to stone
all dead of the flu, 1910 . . .

What difference
with these beasts here
breathing their mass?

Why strive, bend
your bovine body down
and stay, let your animal
instincts overcome,
muzzle full of steaming grass
the black earth piled up —

welcoming beloved earth.

Old Yellow House

Your siding worn the sweetened tone
of a shirt well loved, a poem written
by existence itself as weather works
the skins of things.

Return to your mute decay
that somehow speaks of life.

Beams still strong for the freeborn
swallows, their nests a decade high
above the lintel, where plaster dust
falls into sand.

Your floors still strong
for cows to stand and watch the rain
in the once pink parlour. Through
the windowless windows look —
a mess of balsam root hill,
little horse all a quiver with newness
while the old cows stand and chew.

Look upon the muscles of the land,
the moving must of it
at full tilt the ongoing world.

Up narrow stairs, the shadows
of pictures still hang, outlines of ancestors.
Kick the rusted door wide, and birds scatter.

A child's bedroom exposed again
to the weight of light.

Where Communism Went Wrong

Chairman Mao
likes to see me naked
as I step from the shower.

Patriarch in the sky
your eyes shine
through the steam.

Below your placid face
the people struggle:
one wants a smoke.
another holds back a child
who wants to chase pigeons,
another looks for a toilet.

But you only have eyes for me,
old poet, conqueror,
ravisher of virginal country girls
while your wife sighs
lonely in the Forbidden City.

It must be here
where theories and idealism end.
Here where the flesh
behind its rough grey cotton
calls its stray children home.

Become Child

You cannot
know
what they see
while spinning
in the garden
blissing on a cookie
following a bug

Yet you must
worried mothers
play again

Root in the forest
with your piglets

Turn over stones
just to see

Taste the mud cakes
and the marigold soup

Return every passionate
I Love You

Walk in the ditch river
beneath the orange umbrella

Put kisses in an envelope

Bury a box
of stars

The Barbie Slaughter

Dear Daughter,
you made me a poem
but I don't know how
to read it.

You girls
performed your violence
ruthlessly,
methodically —
not one doll escaped
with her empty head
or her slender arms.
Even Barbie's sisters
beheaded
and dismembered,
left in a heap
of shocking naked plastic;
too reminiscent
of all the real girls
and women
dead at the hands of men,
piled forgotten
in some metaphorical graveyard.

Too haunting
and I can't sort the threads
(*What's Barbie to me or me to Barbie?*)

But you offered no explanation,
your friends mute too.

So your poem
remains unfinished
and trembling
as the fingers approach,
vapid blue eyes wide.

Clean for Now (or the Housekeeper's Lament)

We leave a trail of filth;
dishes crumbs dirt fluids.

Set it all gleaming;
on spin cycle —
let the hot soapy water rain down
and cleanse.

Living is messy.

The dust settles from outer space.
We cannot stop it.

Attack it
with a wet rag or mop and tomorrow
there it is —
the film of living,
the bathtub ring
of sloughed cells,
the mold on the cheese.

Then the Sisyphian toil
of breath and exhalation,
the waste that forms.
evacuates then forms again.

The weight of it
will bury us eventually, billions
eating messing garbaging spitting snoring

and making tender babes
to turn in turn
to shit, bone,
dust.

Murk

It spills into us
the way it spills
into this valley

Murky Times
the Nordic peoples
call it

When the sun
is being hoarded
by some other place

In my dream the turtle
opens her mouth to sing
before remembering
that she cannot

We sleep face to face
in the coyote yelping
half-moon night

But even that light
doesn't reach us
where we kill
or are killed

waiting for the equinox

Mothership

This is the mothership,
the devoured, devouring island
containing:

all the crude myths of man

nectar and offal

languid whales caressing
the planks of the sea

the unlearned
language of fruitflies

homely rats marking their existence
on the edges of things

our toxic chemistry
discreetly erupting through skin

pleats of fabric
under the weight of sight

the urges of salmon
luck of the predator

toad couplings
under a moonlit arbour

trumpet of the scarlet gilia
locked in wax paper

sunsets and earthquakes
stuffed birds and black lipstick

dance of molecules
and the birth of bacteria

the roar of blood
hushing our own extinction

Pregnant in Winter

Twitchy one, little frog legs
you swim in my cave,
kick the chi ball back to the outer reaches,
twirl round my navel as though
round a maypole.

You can't see this
slow sunset, our earth still gripped
by the long, frozen hush,
or that blood in the deer track:
the shock of it, the burn of it
on the forest's white floor.

Baby, the deer are carrying too;
embryonic calves learning to leap
and run, move like thieves
through buried gardens, scratch
at the snow crust for a blade of grass.

But when I'm heaviest,
burdened with gut and milk and worry
(what will you be half me, half he, all you?)
I think of the male Emperor Penguins
at the South Pole, huddled in the skin-killing cold
and imperturbable dark, no food,
no fish for months on end, just the gash of the wind,
that one egg incubating between stomach and toes.

You are the egg and I am deep winter.
I am the unbroken dark, the slosh of a distant sea.
You are the grainy vision of the future,
lifting thumb to mouth, the white
of your new ribs glowing.

Still-life with Birds

1.

Each splendid junco hopping
so much alive
speaks without speaking
his life laid out simple
tracks in snow

Raven finds blood
and the highest places
Does he dream
or are we all
his hallucinations
camped in that merciless
feathered iris

2.

Cold Snap

Sublime vertigo —
a bird has fallen
dead from its perch
frozen, feet up
like some godforsaken
icon

Frost on the panes
as if a hundred songbirds
committed *hara-kiri*
One chest feather each
left to mark their passage

Inevitably
back to raven
stuffing his face
with bloody snow,
stabbing deeply
for somewhere under it all

is flesh, continuance,
nature's quick
recycling of souls

3.

winter again with its grey pall, lowered sky

the birds abandon us
to sickness and the weight of houses

those light, immediate beings
how can we know them; though the taxidermist
turn them inside out to preserve the corporeal
the winged soul is not
contained in the glass eye

raven stays, free in the hold
of his feathers,
surveying the gloom struck valley,
burnt forest, with neutral conscience,
relishing the branch,
the dead thing to pick at

we must have that animal completeness too,
alert in the act of being,
each pulse of the quickening
bird heart
but how to step out
of all things heaped
upon the essential self:
the mortgages, the meals, the agendas,
the machinery, the cactus plants, the tea,
even these

thoughts

on birds

gone south

Dear Nuthatch

keep me company
The dogs conversing
across ravines
are making me lonely

And the hard
spring-bitten light
begins to reveal
its potentials but also
dead endings:
the self
a blackened stalk

The place I knew so well
why can't I recognize it?
Someone has shifted
the hills and a guzzling giant
has drunk the lake
Trees that were one
became two
Many old ones
fallen to wind
and the woodpecker's drill

Trails once walked
now closed by debris
like this heart
older   meanish
from looking upon too long
the wasting of the world

To walk higher
plant tears along deer ways

There —
old bone
clean and speechless

Residue

There is always residue
dust   ash
whatever turns to powder
in the mouth   after speaking
the native quiet
again
The snow has laid
its insulating arms upon us
We are linked
to one another by saliva and vowels
names and conveniences
There has been poetry
fluttering in my brain for days
but the windows
are locked shut
remember the swallow
battering at the attic window
of the boarded up house
in that so close to ghost town?
It was the only living thing
and it was dying
That great cross-country adventure —
dustbowl faces
sunflower field in a storm
prairie-dog town,
their rodent noses glistening
as we cooked supper
We were different then
before the eyes of animals

we waiver now
want more
than moments

Thank-you

Thank-you for this hatred
I've never had one like it before

It gives me something to chew on
these long insomniac nights

Something to mull in strong spice
fill the house with heady aroma

To melt in gall and serve to guests
unsuspecting mineral

A great filler of silence
The waterfall of it rushes in my ears

Thank-you for this hatred freshly born
a shiny plaything to enjoy

For soon it will be dull tossed away
an old brown core composted to dirt

Just Some Poems About the Moon

I

The harvest moon
that last night
married Cassiopeia
and blasted the universe
with yellow light
sleeps
behind blue curtains
and behind the human
iris with its folly
of not seeing
beyond sight
to the actual fullness
dazzling oneness
of form and emptiness
We seek too much
and are
too little

II

In troubled skies
the moon unhinges
Her glow penetrates
the suburban miasma
bathes the ordinary
streets, causes women
to leave their husbands,
uneasy animals to moan
at our doors
We want to walk on water
lay down our lives
for something larger
than what we know
and even this battered
celestial object

which has hounded the earth
for millennia
seems a likely object
of worship
if to worship
we are inclined

III

It's too pale
that hope —
moon in the wind

Babies in the clouds
I beg them
not to be born

It suits rice wine
such a night
where behind white fabric
all small
things are travelling

Smoke wants in
and the orange candle
martyrs itself
for light to write by

Whose courtesan am I
alone on my happy bench;
only the cat
has impulses, my image
fixed in his electric iris,
fur on end and sparking

He doesn't do poetry
He is

Snow Meditation

who said
"I never eat December snowflakes?"

wondering about that
and whether deer ever
stickouttheirthickpinktongues
to catch snow

wondering about the man
who spent his life photographing
snowflakes —
the one who discovered
no two are alike
No fame or money
only that small fascinating thing —
a knowledge that melts
in the palm

wondering too
about the saying
"no snowflake ever lands
in the wrong place"
how to explain that
to my girl
show her
how snow is composed
of billions of irrepeatable
individual crystals,
like children's faces,
or the vanishing moments
that make
a life

Bovine

Two squared
in a king-sized bed

Waking from a dream

Cows lost in their own field
begin lowing —
wanting some wild thing
to gnash their throats?

In this dream
my dad sells an unsafe nuclear power plant
for huge profit,
says *we'd best liquidate our holdings and run away then*
beyond the arm of the law
but where is that?

Bottom of an icy ocean
wreckage of a hundred planes
they sink silently
the bodies the meal trays
the earphones the shoes
from exploded luggage
children's toys
children
food for fish

There must be something the wind has not taken
something just beyond reach
of human hands

Bones

and has not the wind
whistled us hollow
as that birch log etched
by lovers   wariness lodged
beneath their tongues

Ice all the way
No purchase

Lake breathes anonymous
Surface everywhichway feathered
and below it a monstrous calm

We are fogged in
can't meet each other's eyes
sense some falseness there,
some coy rebuke
Only the stones are true
where they lie

In the white light of winter
the bones of things —
immobile, inadequate structures
branches words femurs

Mind fidgets under its wrap
of snow where deer have left
their calligraphy
Birds settle into the dark
branches

till moon burns through warming
all the tired islands of ice

The worm of spring
twists in its burrow
beneath beneath

Coma

They are but shades, shadows on my eyelids;
all those lean inquisitors
who loom and sometimes weep,
come in for a kiss and press
upon my lips the burning mark of life.

They argue whether I should remain
suspended in my cloud of unknowing.
Body moved on, mind moved on;
not to the uplift of heaven on swanish wings,
nor the barbaric realms of hell, just this
continuous bad black
and white movie. Mother, father,
brother, husband mere fabrications
where I roam now in the wormwood,
in the underbelly, in the deepening folds,
lingering for what conclusion,
for the liquid feed, the revolting mulch of my daily bread,
for my warm urine golden in its sac
held up as a jewel,
the twitches of my eyelids telling too much.

And the stubborn pulse.
The stubborn blood still travelling
having forgotten the reason.

I watch, I watch as scorched brain paths erode;
memories liquify . . . sting of the first kiss, my secret way,
tang of wild strawberries, queasy scoop
of the ferris wheel, vomit
in my mouth, faces darkening,
yellow teeth of death as the beast comes slow,
slow with wicked nothingness
and the sweet halo
of release.

Chekhov For Beginners

"You ask me what life is. That is like asking what a carrot is.
A carrot is a carrot and there's nothing more to know."

— Anton Chekov

He expired
at the terrible age
of forty-four.
A black moth battered
itself against the lampshade.
The champagne the doctor brought
instead of the oxygen tent
popped open
by itself and overflowed.

His memories of the steppe,
deprived of electrical impulse,
died, the last joke he had saved
for Olga, his love
of sleigh-rides and claret.

At least the coughing
was over.

His body, brought home
in an oyster truck, greeted
by a military funeral
intended for someone else,
was laid to rest beside his father,
that brutal, autocratic skeleton.

The rabble threw in their fistfuls
of dust.

All his women wept
and lived into their nineties.

Antosha is no more

Midnight, Midlife

Darkness is signaling
beyond the pane.

I have bad dreams, coyotes
wake me into wilderness
as they reclaim the land; snouting
for corpses in the deep ravines,
following the urine trail
of an old buck

or quickly penetrating,
procreating
under the frigid eye
of the January moon.

Night silence full
of elemental
beginnings,
        skunk prowl
          lisp of mouse.

I wake tired
life
portioned
to porridge and dust,
march along
sensible

and bewildered.

Diefenbaker

It was a lock your keys in the car,
step on dog poop,
no cream in your Boston Cream
day.

Rush hour
and traffic lights on the blink
when old Diefenbaker
floated by; black ghost
of that '68 Pontiac, red leather
interior, where I learned
so many songs.

Twenty years
since we were lovers
and I rode in that boat
with you, wishing for the
sweet moon to take us
"Pontiac and all."

He was his own cosmos
that car.

Your girl is a woman now.
I'm remembering her
red hair backlit
by afternoon light on the
Saskatchewan prairie.

I thought you'd crashed
old Diefenbaker but there he was,
a slow black cloud trailing
the message

that somewhere your arm
with its swallow tattoo
keeps on driving.

The Insomniac Considers the Universe

You lay upon me the smooth weight
of your thigh. In fitful remembrance
I cannot connect the dots
of all the celestial objects, nor recall
how they came to be; strange nurseries
of anti-matter, blackening rings
of magnetic worship,
all the mixed-up science of those who spy
on galaxies; tired physicists just trying to comprehend.
Or those with a passion for pain;
they also lick the black curtain of night,
let the dogs of anxiety gnaw at their temples
until they drop their weight into the final
feathers of sleep. Their sweethearts rise
for yoga and laundry, let the pages turn.
But life cannot travel backwards, remember
the hummingbird that for a moment lingers
at the sweetened throat of fuchsia; all day in motion,
all day gathering and what do they consider
perched in their filmy sleep
while the humans toss their runes
and keep asking
what to do
what to do
with this life

until it's gone.

Paperwhite

All breathing things bend
to the scent and sight

of the forced bulb,
Narcissus Tazetta

preternaturally green
with her coy head of bridal perfume.

Within winter the seed
of spring.

Like this

life shoots out of darkness,
tracks appear on snow

and words arrive
on an empty page.

Catherine Mamo holds an M.F.A. in Creative Writing from the University of British Columbia and has had her work published in numerous literary magazines including *sub-TERRAIN*, *The Fiddlehead*, and *Room of One's Own*. Mamo is a mother of two, a freelance writer, and a part-time librarian living in Peachland, British Columbia.